# THE WHITE HOUSE

BRANCH

BRANCH

# THE WHITE HOUSE

DILLON PRESS
Parsippany, New Jersey

by Paula Guzzetti

**Photo Credits**

The White House: front cover, back cover.

Map by Ortelius Design: 6.

AP/Wide World Photos: 22. John F. Kennedy Library: 42. Reproduced from the collections of the Library of Congress: 38. Maryland Historical Society, Baltimore: 10. The White House: 47, 52. © White House Historical Association: 2-3, 13, 15, 19, 25, 27, 28, 30, 36 (detail), 49, 50, 53, 57, 59, 60, 62, 63.

## Library of Congress Cataloging-in-Publication Data

Guzzetti, Paula
    The White House / by Paula Guzzetti — 1st ed.
      p.   cm. — (Places in American History)
    Includes index.
    ISBN 0-87518-650-5 (LSB). — ISBN 0-382-39175-6 (pkb.)
    1. The White House (Washington, D.C.)—Juvenile literature.
  2. Washington (D.C.)—Buildings, structures, etc.—Juvenile literature.
  3. Presidents—United States—Juvenile literature. I. Title. II. Series.
F204.W5G89 1996
975.3—dc20                                            95-13275

Summary: A chronicle of the White House from the time of its inception in President George Washington's administration to its place in American history today. Includes building and construction details, information about room usage, stories about famous occupants, and up-to-date visitor information.

 Published by Dillon Press,
A Division of Simon & Schuster
299 Jefferson Road, Parsippany, NJ 07054

First Edition

Printed in the United States of America

10 9 8 7 6 5 4 3 2 1

# CONTENTS

# CHAPTER 1

# A LOOK BACK

It was a June day in 1791. President George Washington gazed out over the wild stretch of land that sloped down to the river. What he saw were the marshes and woods of an undeveloped territory. What he imagined were the landscaped gardens and grounds of a stately residence. Surrounding the site would be the busy streets of a new United States capital. And on the spot where he now stood would be the President's House, where all future American Presidents would live.

Today, over two centuries later, the President's House is known officially as the White House. Spacious and grand, it has grown from the 36-room mansion that George Washington envisioned to a

132-room complex. It has withstood storms, political turmoil, war, reconstruction, and fire. And its long and colorful history is both the story of a building and a chronicle of America's past.

The White House saga actually began in 1790, one year before George Washington's historic visit to the site. In July of that year, Congress passed the Residence Act, which outlined plans for the national capital. The city would occupy a ten-square-mile tract of land situated along the banks of the Potomac River between the states of Maryland and Virginia. The area would come to be called Washington, D.C.—*Washington*, in honor of the President, and *D.C.* for District of Columbia, in honor of Christopher Columbus. Along with a capitol building where lawmakers would meet to formulate legislation, the President's House was scheduled for completion by the first Monday in December, 1800. President Washington would oversee the construction. Although he would be out of office by the time the capital was built,

Washington never once wavered in his commitment to the job.

The President began by selecting an architect, a Frenchman named Pierre Charles L'Enfant, whom he described as "better qualified than anyone" to design the new city and its structures. But while L'Enfant's plans for the city's layout met with little opposition, his ideas for a capitol building and a "presidential palace" proved far too grand for many of Washington's colleagues. At the insistence of Thomas Jefferson, Washington's secretary of state, L'Enfant was eventually dismissed, and an open competition for more modest architectural designs was held. Nine designs were submitted for the presidential home, including one by Thomas Jefferson himself. The winning entry was the work of an Irish builder named James Hoban. By 1792, work on the two-story residence was underway.

But there were problems from the start. One of the most troublesome was labor. With America's best workers already employed in the

*James Hoban's design for the President's House*

more developed parts of the country, Washington and his team had to recruit foreigners. Finding the right men took time, and it wasn't until 1794 that six Scottish stonecutters were finally hired.

Housing the laborers was another difficulty. In the mansion's "front yard" and the area immediately across from it, a small city had to be raised to accommodate workers' huts, eating halls, carpenter shops, stoneyards, and sawmills.

In addition, even though the original plans had been greatly scaled down, Jefferson and his followers continued to feel that the presidential home was too "royal." With America's independence from England just 20 years old, any hint of royal grandeur was cause for understandable concern. As a result of these problems, when Washington left office in 1797, the house was far behind schedule. By then, it consisted only of stone walls, a wooden frame for the roof, and empty spaces where the windows would be set.

Had the pace of work quickened, the 1800 deadline might have been met. Instead, in 1799, construction stopped completely, as laborers and funds were shifted over to the Capitol. But that did not stop President John Adams from moving in anyway. What he found on that November day in 1800 was an empty building with "not a single apartment finished." The rooms were drafty and poorly lit. Many had not yet been plastered. And the now splendid East Room was so large and bare that his wife, Abigail, used it to hang laundry!

And yet, signs of the mansion's future stateliness were evident. Calling the site a "beautiful spot," Mrs. Adams also proclaimed that the house was "built for ages to come."

Work on the residence continued during the presidencies of both Thomas Jefferson and James Madison. Then, on an August night in 1814, war with the British sent the entire building up in flames.

Disagreements between the United States and Great Britain over trading rights and the freedom of the seas had led to the War of 1812. With orders to burn America's coastal settlements, troops of British soldiers stormed the capital and set the city, including the presidential home, ablaze. Although advance warning had given President Madison and his wife, Dolley, time to flee, the roof of the mansion and its entire interior were completely destroyed. Only a sudden torrential rainfall saved the exterior walls.

*The East Room during the time of Abigail Adams*

The nation's leaders quickly set about the task of rebuilding. Under the supervision of the original architect, James Hoban, reconstruction of the *white* house, as it was now being called, began in 1815. What had originally taken more than ten years to complete was now reconstructed in just two. By October 1817, the country's fifth President, James Monroe, had moved in.

Except for the famous Gilbert Stuart portrait of George Washington, which Mrs. Madison had managed to save, the building's original furnishings had been destroyed in the 1814 fire. With a congressional allocation of $20,000, President Monroe began to purchase replacements. Many of the chairs, vases, and serving pieces he chose are still in use today.

The years between 1824 and 1860 saw the planting of trees and shrubs on the mansion's

*Gilbert Stuart's 1797 portrait of George Washington. It is the only object left of the building's original furnishings.*

grounds and the installation of indoor plumbing, gas lighting, and central heating. The grand front and back entrances, known as the North and South Porticos, were also completed. The presidential home had now become such a symbol of America's strength that not even the Civil War could interfere with its upkeep. As the North and the South fought a long and bloody battle over slavery and states' rights in the 1860s, Congress continued to allocate funds for the building's maintenance. However, it wasn't until Theodore Roosevelt took office in 1901 that the White House, as it was now officially labeled, underwent its most extensive renovation.

Years of continual rebuilding and use had left the home in a state of disrepair. In addition, as the job of the President grew, more office space was needed. The family living quarters of the White House had also proved too small for the Roosevelt clan, which included not only the President and his wife but also their six lively children. With a congressional allocation of almost half a million dollars, the White House was enlarged, new flooring was set, the first closets were installed, and new presidential offices were built in a West Wing.

To the Roosevelts, forced to live in a temporary dwelling nearby, the work seemed to drag on. Eager to move back, they pressed for the project's speedy completion. As a result the last part of the job was hurried and improperly done. This caused the building's structure to weaken and made future reinforcement an expensive necessity. In addition, the reconstruction had disturbed the hiding places of rodents and pests and had sent them scurrying. Their presence continues to plague White House residents to this day.

Despite these problems the Roosevelts settled into their new home with gusto. As Theodore himself later wrote: "I don't think that any family has ever enjoyed the White House more than we have."

As the twentieth century progressed, other changes to the White House followed. In the years between 1909 and 1942, the famous Oval Office was built, the formal Rose Garden was planted, a third floor was added, the West Wing was enlarged, and the East Wing was constructed.

When the United States entered World War II in 1941, a bomb shelter was installed. Army officials also suggested that the White House be painted black to make it more difficult to target in an aerial attack. But President Franklin Roosevelt feared the effect such a change would have on the nation's morale and opposed the change. The familiar white color would remain, a symbol of America's commitment to freedom and democracy both at home and around the world.

In 1948, during the administration of President Harry Truman, the White House got its most complete renovation. At a cost of $5.5 million and taking four years to complete, the work not only repaired the earlier damage but also made the building more up to date. A new

foundation was laid; new steel framework was
erected within the original walls; modern heating,

*The mansion's gutted interior as it looked during the
Truman renovation*

plumbing, air-conditioning, electrical, and communication systems were added; and the famous Truman Balcony was built into the South Portico. Much of the work was done under the critical eye of the outspoken President, who later complained: "If I could have had charge of the construction it would have been done for half the money and in half the time!" Perhaps Truman's annoyance was due to the fact that he and his family had to spend four years of his term living in Blair House, a government-owned property across from the official presidential home.

Though no major reconstruction has taken place since the 1950s, each new administration has worked to maintain the mansion's history and grandeur and to add its own contemporary touch. In addition to the ongoing redecoration and acquisition of historic furnishings and artifacts, the last decades have seen the installation of a movie theater, bowling alley, swimming pool, and jogging track.

But as the White House strives to keep pace with the present, it also stands as a tribute to America's past. More than any other national structure, the White House symbolizes both tradition and change.

*The Bush and Clinton families at the North Portico on Inauguration Day, January 20, 1993. Chelsea Clinton stoops to pet the Bushes' dog, Millie.*

CHAPTER 2

# A STEP INSIDE

"**W**elcome to your new home!" With these words, spoken at the North Entrance of the White House on January 20, 1993, outgoing President George Bush and his wife, Barbara, greeted the mansion's new residents. The forty-second President of the United States, William Jefferson Clinton; his wife, Hillary; and their 12-year-old daughter, Chelsea, were about to move in. After handshakes and hugs the two families crossed the front landing and disappeared through the North Door. The office of the United States presidency was changing hands.

The North Entrance, one of four entrances to the White House, has been the scene of the smooth transition of presidential residency and power for decades. The same entrance has also served as the chief executive's greeting place for official visitors and special friends. Facing Pennsylvania Avenue, this entrance is the one that gives the building its famous address, 1600 Pennsylvania Avenue.

One floor below the North Door, on the opposite side of the house, is the South Entrance, used by high government officials and foreign diplomats. Opening out onto the South Lawn helicopter pad, it is also the passage used by members of the First Family when they leave on or return from official or private trips. To the left of the South Entrance is the West Door, used by the President and his staff when they travel back and forth between the White House proper and the executive offices in the West Wing. To the right is the East Door, used by guests and public visitors.

Just as each place of entry has a purpose, so too does each floor of the White House. The Ground and First Floors are the public floors, used for official government functions. Here, in

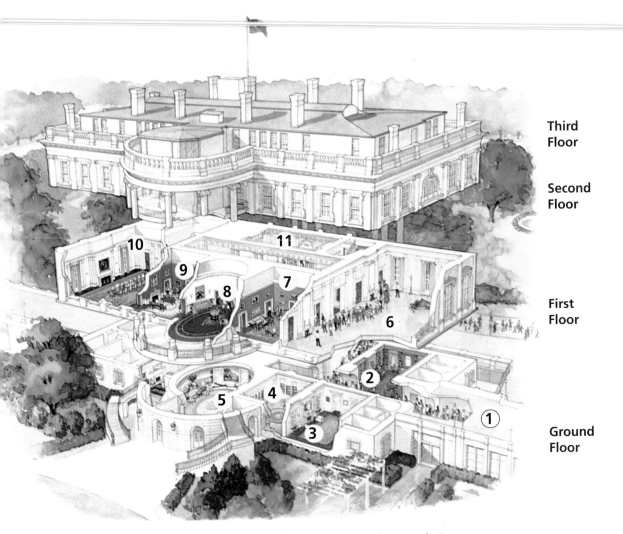

Third
Floor

Second
Floor

First
Floor

Ground
Floor

*A cutaway view of the White House from the South Entrance*

**Ground Floor**
1. East Wing corridor
2. Library
3. Vermeil Room
4. China Room
5. Diplomatic Reception Room

**First Floor**
6. East Room
7. Green Room
8. Blue Room
9. Red Room
10. State Dining Room
11. Entrance Hall

reception rooms, sitting areas, and a State Dining Room, the President and his staff meet and entertain national and foreign leaders. The two lower levels also house the mansion's collection of historic furnishings and artifacts. They are the only floors open to visitors on a regular basis.

The Second and Third Floors are the Family Floors, off-limits to everyone except the President, his family, and invited friends and guests. Consisting of sitting rooms, bedrooms, a dining area, kitchen, and guest quarters, these are the "home" floors on which the First Family actually lives. Since most First Families also retain their previous homes while in the White House, they tend to rely on White House furnishings for the rooms on these floors. It is not unusual, however, for each new set of occupants to add an easy chair, a favorite carpet, or special knickknacks to the government-owned collection.

The most famous rooms of the Family Floors, and the ones that have aroused the most curiosity,

*The West Sitting Hall in the family quarters. This second-floor chamber serves as a private living room for the First Family.*

*The Queens' Suite*

are the guest quarters where many visiting celebrities have been housed. Among these are the Queens' Suite and the notorious Lincoln Bedroom.

The Queens' Suite, named for the royal women who have stayed there, is the most luxurious and popular of the mansion's guest chambers. It includes a small sitting room and bedroom decorated in shades of rose and white, and contains mostly American-made furnishings.

Among its famous treasures is the large canopied bed that once belonged to the nation's seventh President, Andrew Jackson. Its famous occupants have included Queen Elizabeth II of England; her mother, the "Queen Mum"; and her daughter, Princess Anne. The suite has also accommodated nonroyal heads of state, such as foreign presidents and prime ministers, as well as singers, actors, sports figures, and entertainers.

For the more fearless presidential guests, a night in the Lincoln Bedroom might be a spine-chilling adventure. Said to be haunted by Abraham Lincoln's ghost, the room has sent more than one terrified occupant scurrying for cover. Though no one has been able to prove or disprove the ghostly legend, there are some who have reportedly seen or felt Lincoln's "presence" in the room.

Abraham Lincoln, who served as the United States President from 1861 to 1865, never actually slept in the room that bears his name. Like

*The Lincoln Bedroom*

his predecessors, he used the chamber as an office and Cabinet Room. It was there that Lincoln suffered the anguish of the Civil War; signed the Emancipation Proclamation, which freed the slaves; and also mourned the death of his 11-year-old son, Willie. Believers in the Lincoln ghost say that such a caring man could easily have left his larger-than-life spirit behind when he was killed by an assassin's bullet in 1865.

With the White House renovation of 1902, the room that had once served as Lincoln's work place became part of the family living quarters and began to house guests. It was then that furniture from Lincoln's own bedroom was moved in. Not long after, the accounts of ghostly sightings began.

One of the most vivid accounts came from First Lady Grace Coolidge, a White House resident in the 1920s. With admirable calm, the wife of the thirtieth President of the United States described seeing the Lincoln ghost dressed "in black, with a stole draped across his shoulders to ward off the drafts and chills of Washington's night air."

Queen Wilhelmina of the Netherlands, while staying in the Queens' Suite across from the Lincoln Bedroom, had her own frightening encounter with the presidential spirit. Awakened by a knock in the middle of the night, she opened her door to see President Lincoln's figure standing in the hallway. It is said that the queen was so startled that she fainted.

Even some Presidents—Theodore Roosevelt, Harry Truman, Dwight Eisenhower, and George Bush—have reported feeling the Lincoln presence.

Whether it is real, or simply a figment of overactive imaginations, the Lincoln ghost is now part of White House history. Fantasy or fact, it serves as a "living" reminder of our nation's legendary past.

# CHAPTER 3

# Presidents, wives, and Children

"I wonder who lives there," a friend of President Calvin Coolidge once joked, as he and the President were returning to the White House after a walk. "Nobody," was Coolidge's playful reply. "They just come and go."

Forty Presidents have come and gone since the White House first opened its doors at the start of the nineteenth century. Some have stayed only for a few months—others, for as long as eight years; and one, President Franklin Roosevelt, occupied the premises for over a decade! But the White House is never a permanent home for any of its residents. It is a temporary home—to be lived in by each presidential family only for as long as a chief executive holds office.

The Constitution sets the length of each presidential term at four years—a 1951 amendment now limits the number of terms that can be served to just two. That means that at least once or twice in each decade, a new chief executive is sworn in and a new presidential family struggles to adjust to life within the famous white walls. With national attention riveted on the process, each new group of residents is under pressure to establish a personal style and leave a unique and lasting mark.

As the first to occupy the White House, John Adams and his family could do little more than deal with the inconveniences of an unfinished and unfurnished building. Although they moved in just four months prior to the end of President Adams's term, the President and his wife were still expected to host an occasional reception or party. Their entertaining style followed the social customs then fashionable in the courts of Europe. As a result the Adams White House was an unusually formal place—

full of bowing and fine manners but not very much fun.

With the arrival of Thomas Jefferson in 1801, the White House came to life. Parties became smaller and more casual and were focused on comfort and enjoyment rather than on manners or rules. No longer were guests required to bow in greeting, to wait to be served, or to sit at designated places according to social status or rank. Handshakes, serve-yourself dinners, and open seating were now common. President Jefferson, author of the Declaration of Independence, had shown that like all men, all White House guests were created equal.

As a widower, Jefferson often called upon Dolley Madison, wife of his secretary of state, to act as White House hostess. Sociable, lively, and naturally able to make visitors feel at home, Dolley added a warm and feminine touch to official and private White House functions. The experience Dolley gained during the Jefferson era served her well in later years. When her husband

*Dolley Madison, as painted by Gilbert Stuart in 1804*

became President in 1809, Dolley won universal acclaim in her role as First Lady.

The Madison era marked a "golden age" in White House entertaining. For five busy years, the executive mansion sparkled with social events of all kinds. Teas, dinners, banquets, receptions, and parties were the order of the day. Dolley's famous Wednesday evening "drawing rooms," in which the residence was open to the public, were a highlight of the period.

A century later, Theodore Roosevelt and his family took the White House by storm. The most popular and unruly family ever to inhabit the presidential home, they left a mark that no other occupants have matched.

Vigorous, honest, fearless, and strong, Theodore Roosevelt had been a state legislator, a cowboy, a deputy sheriff, a police commissioner, an assistant secretary of the navy, a soldier, the governor of New York, and the vice president of the United States before becoming President at the age of 42. While serving as chief executive, he

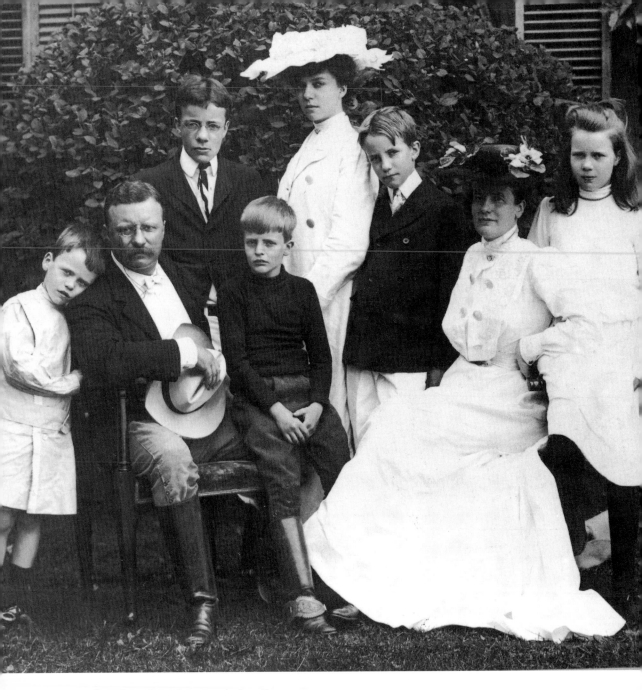

*The Theodore Roosevelt family*

also found time to box, lift weights, play tennis, fence, and practice jujitsu. His five-mile-long "obstacle hikes" became legendary. Scampering over haystacks, fences, and even beach houses, he set new standards for presidential valor. To the distress of the White House staff, he also gave his children some unorthodox ideas for indoor play. Never before, or since, have the mansion's luxuriously upholstered sofas and chairs served as objects on which to play leap-frog!

The White House Gang, as the Roosevelt offspring came to be called, included 17-year-old Alice, 14-year-old Theodore Junior, 11-year-old Kermit, 10-year-old Ethel, 7-year-old Archie, and 3-year-old Quentin. Impossible to harness, the children, their cousins, playmates, and pets could turn up anywhere. A typical day might find the young Roosevelts and their cohorts roller-skating in the corridors, sliding down the stairways on trays, transporting ponies in White House elevators, and walking on stilts through the South Lawn flower beds. No space was off-limits—no act too outrageous to try. Often, the President himself would join in, putting his considerable energy and strength into pillow fights and roughhousing.

"A nervous person had no business around the White House in those days," a staff member later quipped. "He was sure to be a wreck in a very short time."

Mrs. Roosevelt, calm, poised, and smiling, survived the antics of her rambunctious brood by taking a book and disappearing into her sitting room.

White House life took on a more serious tone with the arrival of Franklin Roosevelt in 1933. Disabled by polio, the nation's thirty-second President conducted business from the confines of a wheelchair. In a break with tradition, First Lady Eleanor Roosevelt played an administrative role. Serving as the President's spokesperson, she traveled extensively on his behalf and soon became a respected figure in her own right. As the first presidential wife to hold her own press conferences, to testify before Congress in support of social legislation, and to work for world peace and human rights, Eleanor Roosevelt became known as the First Lady of the World. In light of her busy schedule, it is not surprising that hot-dog picnics sometimes replaced the stately White House banquets of the past.

With the 1960s came a new era of White House elegance and charm. The election of John F. Kennedy at the start of the decade gave the nation a young and handsome President and, in Jacqueline Bouvier Kennedy, a beautiful and cultured First Lady. Interested in history and the arts, the Kennedys did much to enliven the mansion's appearance and mood. From the historic restoration of White House rooms to East Room concerts, poetry readings, and plays to gala receptions for the leading artists and writers of the day, the Kennedys added a unique magic and sparkle.

In addition, the Kennedy children—three-year-old Caroline and two-month-old John Junior—were often photographed during their White House playtimes. To millions of Americans, John Junior will forever be a little boy peeking out from under his father's desk in the Oval Office.

Under President Clinton in the 1990s, the White House has taken both a step back and a giant leap forward. Reminiscent of Franklin and Eleanor Roosevelt, the new President and First Lady are working side by side on the important issues of the day. But they have taken the Roosevelt example one step further. Shortly after his election, President Bill Clinton appointed First Lady Hillary Rodham Clinton to head his Task Force on Health Care. A lawyer and activist, Hillary Clinton is the first presidential wife to operate from an office in the

*John Kennedy Jr. in his "house," as he called the space under the President's desk*

executive West Wing. The move from the socially-oriented East Wing, the traditional First Lady domain, has placed Hillary close to the center of power. This move seems to say that the Dolley Madison days are now past. In the Clinton White House, as in the nation, the age of feminism has arrived.

# CHAPTER 4

# THE NATION'S BUSINESS

The year was 1968. America was involved in a difficult and costly war in Vietnam. The American people were increasingly divided over whether United States troops should stay and fight, or pull out and return home. As opposition mounted, mobs of angry protesters took to the streets in massive antiwar demonstrations. On the evening of March 31, as antiwar pickets lined up along the White House gates, President Lyndon Johnson addressed the nation in a televised speech from the Oval Office:

> This country's ultimate strength lies in the unity of our people. There is a division in the American house. Accordingly, I shall not seek, and I will not accept, the

nomination of my party for another term as your President.

This dramatic and startling announcement by the President was made from the White House Oval Office, the true hub of the United States presidency since 1909.

One of four oval rooms in the White House complex—the Blue Room, the Diplomatic Reception Room, and the Yellow Oval Room are the other three—the Oval Office is located at the southeastern end of the West Wing. Joined to the main part of the house by a covered walkway, it is within easy walking distance of the family quarters, the first-floor state rooms, and nearby staff offices. Like the living quarters, it is off-limits to visitors except by special invitation. Regular access by the press, however, has made it one of the mansion's most recognized interiors.

With constitutional authority to make treaties; to appoint ambassadors, public ministers, and

*The Oval Office*

judges; and to command the armed forces, the President is the chief formulator of national and foreign policy. Working with legislators, judges, Cabinet members, and staff, the President sets the nation's course and oversees the handling of its affairs. The work space and sitting areas of the Oval Office provide convenient places for decision-making, clerical tasks, small meetings, and public broadcasts.

When larger or more formal settings are necessary, work can move out to other rooms in the West Wing, including the Cabinet Room. Used for meetings with heads of the various government departments, the Cabinet Room is dominated by an oval-shaped conference table that can seat up to 18 people. Here, the nation's education, economy, national defense, foreign policy, health, housing, labor, and agriculture are given top-level attention.

For daily staff meetings, the nearby Roosevelt Room might be the presidential chamber of choice. Named by President Richard Nixon in

*The Cabinet Room*

*The Roosevelt Room*

honor of Theodore Roosevelt, the room also occasionally doubles as a press conference site.

Presidential meetings with the press have been an important feature of White House life since the days of Theodore Roosevelt. A vital link between the chief executive and the people, the press gained official White House recognition with the addition of the West Wing Press Lobby in 1969. Complete with work areas and broadcast booths, the Lobby also houses a Press Briefing Room. Here, the President and his spokespeople issue daily reports on the status of national affairs. These presidential updates form the basis of the White House news stories that are printed in periodicals and broadcast on radio and television throughout the world.

More formal press conferences are usually held in the East Room. The biggest of the mansion's reception areas, it is largely unfurnished and can easily accommodate scores of journalists and reporters. Since they are usually televised, East Room press conferences, like Oval

*The President's office in the family quarters. Once used for the signing of treaties, the chamber is still sometimes called The Treaty Room.*

*The Rose Garden*

Office broadcasts, provide a way for the President to communicate more directly with the nation he serves.

America's chief executive may sometimes choose to work "at home." There are rooms on the Family Floors that are easily converted to offices for administrative use.

And on fine days, business may even be conducted outdoors. The Rose Garden, just outside the Oval Office, makes an ideal setting for many presidential tasks. From press conferences and meetings with foreign leaders to official ceremonies and state dinners, the Rose Garden has become an important extension of the executive West Wing. Resplendent with chrysanthemums in autumn, tulips and hyacinths in spring, and the summer roses that give it its name, the Rose Garden is the perfect spot to combine presidential business with pleasure.

# CHAPTER 5

# THE PEOPLE'S HOUSE

Before he left office in 1837, President Andrew Jackson received an unusual gift. A New York cheese maker, who was also a loyal supporter, sent him a chunk of cheddar. No ordinary sample, this presidential version weighed a whopping 1,400 pounds and measured 4 feet in diameter and 2 feet in depth. What did Jackson do with his colossal-sized snack? The "People's President," living in the "People's House," invited the people to share it.

With the giant cheddar stationed in a place of prominence in the White House Entrance Hall, the President opened the mansion's doors to the public. Within seconds, dozens of curious and excited citizens rushed in, eager to grab a tasty bite. Tearing away at the cheese, they left a crumbly mess behind. Bits of cheddar and splotches of grease were embedded in carpets, upholstery, and floors. It took weeks of work before the oily stains faded and the smell of cheddar disappeared.

Today, over a century and a half later, the "People's House" is still open to the public but in a much more orderly manner. The only residence of a head of state that allows regular public access, the White House welcomes citizens and foreign visitors to public receptions, South Lawn Easter-egg hunts, and seasonal garden tours. And for more than 1.5 million men, women, and children each year, White House tours offer a first-hand glimpse inside.

Self-guided tours begin at the building's East Entrance. Visitors make their way along the Ground Floor Corridor, passing the Library, which houses a collection of reference volumes and American classics, and the Vermeil Room, where silver tableware is displayed. Mounting

*The East Room*

the stairs, they ascend to the First Floor for a
look at the five historic State Rooms.

The East Room, which is the most formal of
the five rooms, looks much as it did after the

1902 renovation. Dazzling the eye with gold and white decorations and chandeliers, this chamber makes a perfect setting for large gatherings. In addition to official functions, the room also serves as a private party area for the First Family. Two of the best-known events held here include the 1906 wedding of Alice Roosevelt and the 1970s senior prom of President Gerald Ford's daughter, Susan. Along the east wall is the famous portrait of George Washington by artist Gilbert Stuart— the same painting that Dolley Madison saved from the fire of 1814.

Adjacent to the East Room is the Green Room, named for the predominant color of its furnishings. Decorated in a style that was popular during America's early years, the room serves as a reception and sitting area. Most of the furniture in the room was crafted by Duncan Phyfe, a famous nineteenth-century American cabinetmaker. The paintings on the silk-covered walls include scenes of nineteenth-century American life and are among the most prized in the mansion's collection.

*The Green Room*

*The Blue Room*

The oval-shaped Blue Room, considered by many to be the most beautiful room in the White House, is colored in tones of white, gold, and blue. It contains many pieces of furniture purchased by President Monroe after the 1814 fire. Overlooking the South Lawn, the room offers a breathtaking view of the Washington Monument and the Jefferson Memorial. The chamber serves as a reception area and also houses the White House tree at Christmas.

The Red Room, a favorite of First Ladies, is used as a reception space and sitting area. True to its name, it is almost completely red, from its satin walls to its sofas, armchairs, and rosewood tables. The Red Room is famous as the site of Dolley Madison's Wednesday-night receptions. In tribute, Dolley's portrait, also by Gilbert Stuart, hangs on the chamber's north wall.

Next to the Red Room is the State Dining Room, scene of luncheons, teas, and as many as 30 formal dinners each year. Large enough to

*The Red Room*

*The State Dining Room, set for a formal function*

accommodate 140 guests, it is located one floor
above the White House kitchens, where highly
skilled chefs prepare sumptuous fare. During
gala occasions, the State Dining Room is aglow
with candles, fresh flowers, and sparkling tableware from the mansion's historic collection of

presidential china. Carved into the mantel, just below a portrait of President Lincoln, are the words of the building's first occupant, John Adams:

> I Pray Heaven to Bestow the Best of Blessings on THIS HOUSE and on All that shall hereafter Inhabit it. May none but Honest and Wise Men ever rule under this Roof.

The tour ends in the Entrance Hall. Often used as an informal ballroom, the Entrance Hall also houses painted portraits of America's most recent Presidents. To the left of the doorway is the much-photographed Grand Staircase, which links the State Floor to the Family Floor above. Here on red-carpeted marble stairs, the President and First Lady pose for official White House photographs with their most honored White House guests.

For many visitors who pass through the White House's splendid and timeless rooms, a special feeling will linger. Is it a new sense of the past? Is it a clearer understanding of America's present and future? Or is it simply an appreciation for a structure that is as old and enduring as our democracy itself? Majestic and proud, the White House stands rooted in tradition yet ever open to change. As a symbol of America's Presidents and people, it is a powerful and stirring sight.

# THE WHITE HOUSE: A HISTORICAL TIME LINE

**1789**  George Washington becomes the first U.S. President.

**1790**  Congress passes the Residence Act, outlining plans for a national capital, Washington, D.C., that will include a capitol building and a President's house. George Washington is chosen to oversee construction.

**1791**  Washington selects Pierre Charles L'Enfant  to design the capital, including the Capitol building and the presidential residence.

**1792**  L'Enfant is dismissed. James Hoban's design for the President's House is accepted and work begins.

**1797**  President Washington leaves office.

**1799**  Construction on the President's House temporarily stops.

**1800**  President John Adams moves into the unfinished building in November.

**1800–1814**  Work on the house continues.

**1814**  British soldiers set fire to the house—only its outer walls remain.

**1815**  Reconstruction begins.

**1817**  President James Monroe moves into the rebuilt structure and refurnishes it.

**1824**  The South Portico is built.

**1825– 1837**  The residence's grounds are planted under Presidents John Quincy Adams and Andrew Jackson.

**1829**  The North Portico is built.

**1833**  Indoor plumbing is installed.

**1848**  Gas lighting is added.

**1853**  Central heating is installed.

**1861– 1865**  America fights the Civil War. President Lincoln signs the Emancipation Proclamation freeing the slaves on January 1, 1863.

**1901**  The President's House is officially renamed the White House.

**1902**  The building is enlarged, the first closets are built, and the West Wing is constructed.

**1909**  The Oval Office is built in the West Wing.

**1913**  The Rose Garden is planted.

**1927**   A third floor is added.

**1933**   An indoor swimming pool is built. (It is replaced by an outdoor pool in 1975.)

**1941**   The East Wing is constructed. The United States enters World War II. A bomb shelter is installed.

**1942**   A movie theater is added in the East Wing.

**1948–1952**   The White House undergoes a major renovation. Modern heating, plumbing, air-conditioning, electrical, and communications systems are added. The Truman Balcony is built into the South Portico.

**1949**   Bowling lanes are installed in the West Wing. (They are moved to the residence area in 1973.)

**1961**   Historic restoration of White House rooms takes place under the Kennedys.

**1969**   A Press Lobby is added in the West Wing.

**1993**   A jogging track is built on the White House grounds.

# PRESIDENTS

| | | | |
|---|---|---|---|
| George Washington | 1789–1797 | Benjamin Harrison | 1889–1893 |
| John Adams | 1797–1801 | Grover Cleveland | 1893–1897 |
| Thomas Jefferson | 1801–1809 | William McKinley | 1897–1901 |
| James Madison | 1809–1817 | Theodore Roosevelt | 1901–1909 |
| James Monroe | 1817–1825 | William H. Taft | 1909–1913 |
| John Quincy Adams | 1825–1829 | Woodrow Wilson | 1913–1921 |
| Andrew Jackson | 1829–1837 | Warren G. Harding | 1921–1923 |
| Martin Van Buren | 1837–1841 | Calvin Coolidge | 1923–1929 |
| William Henry Harrison | | Herbert Hoover | 1929–1933 |
| | 1841–1841 | Franklin D. Roosevelt | |
| John Tyler | 1841–1845 | | 1933–1945 |
| James K. Polk | 1845–1849 | Harry S. Truman | 1945–1953 |
| Zachary Taylor | 1849–1850 | Dwight D. Eisenhower | |
| Millard Fillmore | 1850–1853 | | 1953–1961 |
| Franklin Pierce | 1853–1857 | John F. Kennedy | 1961–1963 |
| James Buchanan | 1857–1861 | Lyndon B. Johnson | 1963–1969 |
| Abraham Lincoln | 1861–1865 | Richard M. Nixon | 1969–1974 |
| Andrew Johnson | 1865–1869 | Gerald R. Ford | 1974–1977 |
| Ulysses S. Grant | 1869–1877 | Jimmy Carter | 1977–1981 |
| Rutherford B. Hayes | 1877–1881 | Ronald Reagan | 1981–1989 |
| James A. Garfield | 1881–1881 | George Bush | 1989–1993 |
| Chester A. Arthur | 1881–1885 | William Jefferson Clinton | |
| Grover Cleveland | 1885–1889 | | 1993– |

# VISITOR INFORMATION

## WASHINGTON D.C.

### Hours

10:00 A.M. to noon, Tuesday through Saturday. Closed
Sunday, Monday, some holidays, and for official
functions.

### Self-Guided Tours

Self-guided tours are free. However, tickets are
necessary during the peak season between
Memorial Day and Labor Day. They may be
obtained at the ticket booth on the Ellipse, just
south of the White House. Tickets are distributed
on a first-come, first-served basis and show the
approximate time of the tour. They are valid only
on the day issued. Ticket booth hours are 8:00 A.M.
to noon, Tuesday through Saturday. Lines are
usually long and form early.

During the off-peak season, visitors line up at the
East Gate of the White House. Those in line
before noon are usually admitted.

Self-guided tours may take between 20 and 35
minutes and include a walk past the Library and
Vermeil Room on the Ground Floor and a walk
through the five State Rooms on the First Floor.

## Guided Tours

Guided tours are also free but require reservations. Visitors can obtain reserved tickets by writing to their representative in the United States House or Senate six to eight weeks in advance of the visit. Guided tours take place at 8:15, 8:30, and 8:45 A.M., Tuesday through Saturday. In addition to the rooms open for the self-guided tour, guided tours may also include the China Room and the Diplomatic Reception Room on the Ground Floor. Guided tours take between 35 and 50 minutes. Tickets are extremely limited, so it is best to list alternate dates when writing.

## Special Events

Tours can be delayed or canceled without notice for official events. For the most up-to-date information on daily events, call the White House Visitors' Office Tour Line at (202) 456-7041.

For information on spring and fall garden tours and other special events, call (202) 456-2200.

## Additional Information

For other information, telephone the White House Visitors' Office at (202) 456-7041.

# INDEX